THE ART OF CONVERSATION

HOW TO TALK TO ANYONE, ANYWHERE, ANYTIME, AND OVERCOME SHYNESS AND SOCIAL ANXIETY

JIM ALEXANDER

© **Copyright 2022 - All rights reserved.**

The content contained within this book may not be reproduced, duplicated, or transmitted without direct written permission from the author or the publisher.

Under no circumstances will any blame or legal responsibility be held against the publisher, or author, for any damages, reparation, or monetary loss due to the information contained within this book, either directly or indirectly.

Legal Notice:

This book is copyright protected. It is only for personal use. You cannot amend, distribute, sell, use, quote, or paraphrase any part, or the content within this book, without the author or publisher's permission.

Disclaimer Notice:

Please note that the information contained within this document is for educational and entertainment purposes only. All effort has been executed to present accurate, up-to-date, reliable, complete information. No warranties of any kind are declared or implied. Readers acknowledge that the author is not rendering legal, financial, medical, or professional advice. The content within this book has been derived from various sources. Please consult a licensed professional before attempting any techniques outlined in this book.

By reading this document, the reader agrees that under no circumstances is the author responsible for any losses, direct or indirect, that are incurred due to the use of the information in this document, including, but not limited to, errors, omissions, or inaccuracies.

CONTENTS

Introduction   5

1. The Problem of Shyness and Social Anxiety   15
2. The Art of Conversation   23
3. Strategies to Overcome the Fear of Talking with Others   29
4. How to Know What to Say in Any Situation or Environment   39
5. How to Have an Amazing Conversation in 7 Steps   47
6. Tips for Asking Questions and Listening Well   57
7. Dealing with Difficult Situations   63

Conclusion   73

INTRODUCTION

I struggled to talk to people, especially in daily life. I would avoid eye contact at all costs and even break out into sweat or shake nervously when somebody approached me. Talking was the very last thing on my mind for that first two years of college. One day, I decided enough is enough. If I don't speak up now, then who will? So I started to try, and it didn't work out for me very well. To be frank, I was very socially awkward after my first few attempts. But you know what? This isn't a death sentence because there is a solution: conversation practice.

I've been practicing conversation for over three years now with a lot of success, and this book will show you how to do the same.

Conversations are everywhere in life whether we realize it or not. If we lived in an isolated society with no other people around, then conversations would never happen except between ourselves in our own minds. Thankfully, that is not the world we live in right now! If you want to chat up anybody from your family members to complete strangers on the street, then you will have to learn how to talk. This book will show you exactly how to do that.

Starting with the basics of what conversation actually is and why it's important, this book will help you overcome your fears in order to speak up more often. Being shy doesn't mean that you can't talk or that people will reject you. It just means that you have some self-doubt, which this book will get rid of immediately. You will learn how to think about your partner in conversation so that they are more engaged with the words that come out of your mouth. This is a skill that will give you great fulfillment because it opens up new social possibilities everywhere you go.

Loneliness has now surpassed obesity as the number one health epidemic in the United States.

Young people under the age of 21 feel the impact of loneliness most severely. A reason for this is that they use technology as an excuse to avoid face-to-face interactions, and don't learn how to carry a conversation outside of social media sites like Facebook or Instagram. According to recent statistics, one in five millennials has no friends. And a poll conducted in 2020 found that 71 percent of millennials and almost 79 percent of Gen Z respondents felt lonely, which was considerably more than other generations. According to the AARP Public Policy Institute, approximately 42.6 million adults over the age of 45 in the United States feel lonely, and roughly half of those people report that their loneliness has increased over time.

According to a survey conducted by Cigna Corporation in 2017, Gen Z and Millennials have seven times more anxiety than Baby Boomers do when meeting new people. Also, adults under 25 are three times as likely to report feeling alone in an average day than those over 55 years old.

In the past decade, the number of people who admitted they sometimes or always felt lonely has doubled from 11% to 22%. In fact, it is estimated that 50% of the population will experience some degree of loneliness at least once in their lifetime.

People who report feeling lonely typically have less social connections and interactions with others. Loneliness is also associated with poorer sleep quality, cardiovascular disease, cognitive decline, Alzheimer's disease and dementia, depression, suicide attempts among adolescents, and impaired immune systems.

There are 7 billion people on Earth, but it feels like there are no people in your life. It could be you don't have many friends, or your best friend moved away to college leaving you alone. Or maybe you've recently moved to a new city and haven't made any friends yet. Loneliness is very powerful when not dealt with right away, because it can lead to severe health issues including addiction, obesity, heart disease, and depression.

We are inherently social beings that crave connections to others. Having the skills to initiate meaningful interactions with others can strengthen our relationships, boost our professional lives, and bring us more satisfaction day-to-day.

When it comes to building connections, most of us are very good at meeting new people but have a harder time making an impact with them. Even if we do start a conversation, it takes effort on both parts to keep it going. We wonder how many opportunities we've missed because we couldn't think of anything interesting enough to say beyond small chat. This book will provide practical applications so you can approach people with confidence in any environment and use their observations of you (and your surroundings) as springboards for deeper conversations.

You don't need special talent or even like some form of social butterfly to start conversations with people in your daily life. All you need is the willingness to put yourself out there and some basic acting skills, which are gained by practice (like any other skill).

I was that person. Shy, withdrawn, and always preferring to stay in the shadows. I never talked to anyone unless I had to. And even then, it was always a struggle.

Then one day, I decided to change things. I went out and started striking up conversations with strangers. And you know what? It was terrifying at first, but it also felt exhilarating. I was finally breaking out of my shell and experiencing the world firsthand.

It wasn't easy, but with time I got better at it. I started making friends, and my social life flourished.

The best part? I no longer felt alone or isolated. Conversations became a way for me to connect with people and learn a little bit about them from the inside out. And that made me feel great about myself, because I could share interests and get to know someone better in a short amount of time.

The Art of Conversation is the book I wish I had when I was younger. It's a simple, practical guide that shows you how to truly connect with anyone. From construction workers to your neighbor next door, this book is full of ways to start conversations that are interesting and engaging.

This book is for anyone who wants to have more meaningful conversations with others. It doesn't matter if you're shy or outgoing, this book will give you the tools you need to connect with others in any situation. Whether you're at a party, work, or school, this book will help you feel more comfortable talking to people and make lasting connections.

This book is not for people who are already confident in their social skills. This book is for people who want to build up their confidence and learn how to have meaningful conversations with others.

- Are you tired of not knowing what to say?

- Do you wish you had more friends?
- Is it frustrating that you always get the wrong people because there's not enough time for small talk?
- Do you want to improve your conversational skills so that way it'll be easier to make friends or network professionally?
- Are you tired of spending hours on end at home alone because everyone else seems busy and unfriendly (or worse, obnoxious) all the time?
- Do you want more people to approach you, instead of having to work so hard at being outgoing?
- Do you want people to take an interest in you and what you have to say?
- Are you ready for the transformation to take place within you?

Then "The Art of Conversation" is for you. Imagine how amazing it will feel to know exactly what to say and do around anyone, anytime, anywhere. Imagine having your personality draw people in and making it easier for others to talk to you. Imagine meeting your soulmate and making him or her feel instantly comfortable around you. With

"The Art of Conversation", that fantasy can become reality.

A skeptic would say that it is not possible to talk to anyone with ease because it takes a lot of practice and effort to be able to do so. They would also say that it is not possible to read someone's mind and know what they are thinking or feeling. Fortunately, they would be wrong. In fact, it is possible to talk to anyone with ease by simply understanding how the brain functions in social situations.

If you are concerned you will always be shy, the answer is you won't be. This comes with practice, not only reading the book and stopping there. The entire book is laid out for you step-by-step on how to speak to people in various circumstances. After you learn these basic concepts, all it takes is will power to implement them until they become second nature.

This book is still for you even if you are not scared of starting conversations. You can easily take these ideas to any party or other social setting you want by being more sociable, making friends, and having interesting stories to relate to people. Even further than that, this book will teach you how to become more assertive with your wants and needs. You will be able to get what you feel like you deserve in all parts of your life, whether it is a raise at work or the love you deserve.

How This Book Is Different

1. This book provides practical applications that can be used immediately.
2. It is not just about making small talk, but rather having meaningful conversations with anyone.
3. It does not rely on theoretical concepts, but instead on real-world observations and experiences.

How To Read This Book

The best way to read this book in order to overcome shyness would be to take it slow. Don't try to do everything all at once. Start by reading one chapter at a time and then applying the tips that are given. Be patient with yourself and don't get discouraged if you don't see results right away. It takes time and practice to overcome shyness.

The process of overcoming shyness is built around the idea that by having more conversations with people, you will feel more comfortable and confident in conversation. As we read earlier, socializing helps to build up our immune system and protects us against stress and illness. So not only does it help your mental health, but also your physical health as well.

1

THE PROBLEM OF SHYNESS AND SOCIAL ANXIETY

The problem with being shy and socially anxious is that it can be difficult to experience life. In fact, you might not even have a chance to meet the person who could change your life for the better because you're too afraid of being around people. You might feel like there's no hope for a happy future. But this feeling isn't true - there are many things you can do right now to start improving your social skills and make progress on getting out of this lonely place. The first step is understanding what shyness really is, why it happens, and how it impacts your feelings about yourself as well as other people's feelings about you.

The Problem with Being Shy

Shyness is a common condition for many adults and children as well as adolescents (for some people it continues into adulthood, while others simply grow out of it). It's characterized by feeling nervous, self-conscious, or tense when you're in social situations. Your heart beats faster than normal, you may tremble slightly, your arms and legs feel less steady - all physical signs that something is making you uncomfortable. You might feel like you have nothing to say to the person you are speaking with even though this isn't true. But because your brain seems to be stuck on how shy and awkward you feel around other people, these thoughts make it difficult for you to speak freely.

Shy people usually know that their shyness is a problem because it makes them feel awkward, nervous, and self-conscious. They become so preoccupied with being afraid of what others think about them that they can't enjoy or learn from social situations. They also have a hard time meeting new people. They believe the worst - that other people won't want to be around them because they feel nervous and uncomfortable in social settings.

What Causes Social Anxiety?

The cause of social anxiety varies from person to person. Your overall temperament (whether you're more introverted or extraverted) may play a role in how socially anxious you are - all children will experience some level of shyness at some point, but if these feelings last into adolescence and don't go away as your brain develops, you may have a more severe form of social anxiety.

However, genetics and life experiences can also contribute to feeling shy and socially anxious. For example, if a family member is shy or isolated, this may make you feel as though it's not safe to open up around other people. You might subconsciously feel that trying harder to overcome your shyness will damage relationships with family members since they share the same feelings about socializing.

Or perhaps another person made fun of you when you were growing up because of how you acted in social situations. If so, you might believe that there's something wrong with you - which is why it's so hard for people who are shy and socially anxious to build self-confidence and feel good about themselves.

What are the Negative Effects of Shyness and Social Anxiety?

Shyness is a common condition that causes many people to suffer emotionally in social situations. You may feel like you want to meet friends, but when it comes time to take steps in this direction, you shut down because your shyness makes it difficult for you to maintain eye contact or speak up when around other people. This can make you feel like there's something wrong with you - which means that even if others don't react negatively when they see how uncomfortable you act in social settings, YOU might hold onto the belief that YOU are the reason no one wants to be around YOU. And since research shows that people who have low self-esteem also have low social esteem, this can cause you to feel even more hesitant and insecure around other people - creating further isolation.

These negative effects on your life don't just include emotional consequences. There are also some substantial physical consequences of shyness and social anxiety that you need to be aware of, including:

- an increased risk for heart disease (which

might be the result of heart palpitations, tension headaches, chest pain, and other physical symptoms that can occur when you're anxious)
- a greater chance of developing immune system problems (since being stressed for a long period of time can weaken your immune system)
- being more likely to suffer from respiratory diseases such as asthma (and research has also found that the symptoms of respiratory diseases are more likely to be severe for individuals who are shy or socially anxious)
- the possibility of being diagnosed with chronic fatigue syndrome, irritable bowel syndrome, and fibromyalgia (since people who are shy are more likely to have an existing physical condition such as one of these disorders).

Can social anxiety lead to feelings of loneliness?

As mentioned before, people who are shy and socially anxious often feel like there's something wrong with them. This can lead to feelings of loneliness because you may be left out of social gatherings, family get-togethers, or other events that require connecting with others on some level. You might even try to avoid these situations because they make you uncomfortable - but this can lead to even more isolation and loneliness.

How does shyness affect social skills?

Shy people often say they feel like they don't know how to act around other people, and also that it's difficult for them to meet new friends of the opposite sex. But just because you think there might be something wrong with you, this doesn't mean there IS something wrong with you. In fact, research shows that shyness is a very common trait - and because it's so common, there are likely many people just like you who have the same feelings about socializing as you do.

What can I do to eliminate my shyness?

If you're a person who is shy and doesn't like the way it affects your life, you may be wondering if there's anything you can do to change how you feel in social situations. The good news is that research does show that people who are shy can make changes on their own without having to go through counseling or any type of therapy.

But before getting into these changes, let me warn you that if you try to just force yourself to change how you react in social environments without doing the proper work on your self-esteem and self-image, you won't be successful at overcoming shyness.

In fact, this often creates a vicious cycle of feeling awkward in social settings, trying to push yourself to act differently and failing, and undermining your self-esteem even more.

So yes, you need to make changes in how you feel about yourself in order to change how you behave when interacting with others. And don't worry - there are many things you can do to improve yourself which will make it much easier for you to stop feeling shy when you're around other people.

So, how can you work on eliminating shyness in your life? The first step is to accept that it's normal to feel shy sometimes - and that many people feel the same way. Second, understand that change will not happen overnight, so be patient with yourself as you work through the different steps involved in overcoming shyness. Third, make sure you're focusing on building a positive self-image and healthy self-esteem; this is essential if you want to be successful at changing how you react around other people. Fourth, focus on developing social skills by practicing in safe environments where you feel comfortable. Finally, don't try to force yourself to change how you behave around others without doing the proper work on your self-image.

There are many changes you can make to eliminate shyness from your life - and although it will take some time, the effort will be worth it.

2

THE ART OF CONVERSATION

A conversation is an art form, and it requires a significant amount of skill. This may sound like a strange idea at first, but when you think about it, the conversation is very similar to other forms of communication such as dance or theater. Many different aspects go into making a good conversation: the words we use, how we say them, and what our body language communicates in response all play important roles in determining whether or not we have succeeded in communicating effectively with another person. The more skilled you become at any form of communication (including conversation), the easier it becomes to do well. It also makes sense that many people who excel at these other forms choose careers where they can practice their skills on a regular basis; for example, an actor becomes an expert at dialogue and body language through repeated practice; a dancer learns to read and memorize the choreography of every dance they are assigned to perform. This is just as true for conversation as well, whether you are using it in your professional life or simply having casual chats with friends that last an hour or two.

Why do people have conversations?

There are many reasons to have a conversation. Sometimes conversations happen because people share common interests and they want to explore them together in greater depth. Other times, it is simply an excuse to spend time with each other in a relaxed setting, where no work or demands are involved. However, the most practical use of conversation comes when it's used as a means of exchanging information - be it between two friends discussing what restaurants they've tried lately or an executive telling her assistant about the upcoming meeting she has scheduled that afternoon.

Conversation Skills

So what makes for a good conversation? Conversation skills can be broken down into four areas:

content, delivery style, body language, and writing style. Good content includes having something interesting or useful to say and saying it in an organized manner. Delivering your content the right way requires having good timing, knowing when to speak up and when to be quiet, how loud or soft you should speak, and what tone you should use (sarcastic, serious, humorous, etc). Good body language includes maintaining eye contact with the other person without staring at them (this can come across as aggressive), leaning forward slightly while they talk to show interest in what they're saying, and nodding periodically so they know you're following along.

Some people may naturally have these skills better than others, but in most cases, you can learn them if you put in the time to practice. And it's not hard to practice either - with cell phones and laptops at our disposal these days, there are many opportunities we get throughout the day to review what we've said and how we said it. The next time someone asks for your email address so they can send out a presentation you worked on together, ask them to give you some feedback on how well the meeting went. Or when someone says something that catches your attention or sparks an idea for a new project, ask yourself: "What did they say that made me think of this?" and write down what specifically stood out. This way you will become more aware of what makes a good conversation and how different people communicate, which gives you the tools to further develop your skills.

Learning a new language is difficult enough as it is. Imagine trying to do so with no prior experience or skills in that language! The Art of Conversation shares many of the same basic principles as learning a foreign language: for example, being aware of what works and doesn't work when having a conversation helps you be more successful at conveying ideas between people who speak different languages. In both cases, awareness is key. Once you understand not only your own strengths but also the other person's preferences, you have all the information needed to adjust your conversational approach accordingly. For instance, if someone asks how your day was and you tell them in a way that implies this is just another mundane day, they will no doubt walk away uninterested. On the other hand, if you take time to point out what made your day interesting or exciting, or even one thing that was particularly difficult but you managed to get through it successfully, this person might want to hear more from you in the future.

The Art of Conversation is a simple skill that takes time to develop but can have far-reaching benefits for those who put in the effort to learn it. So set aside some time each week for this worthy endeavor and before long you'll be having great conversations with everyone around you - even complete strangers!

3

STRATEGIES TO OVERCOME THE FEAR OF TALKING WITH OTHERS

It is natural for people to be scared of speaking to one another. This fear is not just related to social anxiety, but also has roots in our evolution. For most of human history, the size of a tribe was about 150 members or less. And in order to survive in this type of environment, you had to know everyone else in your tribe intimately. You couldn't afford any enemies because they could kill you and take over everything that belonged to you with ease. Say one wrong word, and the tribal leader would kill you! Especially if you were a man trying to talk to a female. But now we're in the modern world where we have a sense of anonymity. There's no need to know everyone by name or face, and most of us feel very little threat from strangers because the world has become so huge.

We are now able to make small talk with ease if we choose to do so, but many people still struggle with it - particularly students around the age of puberty. This is the time that many people begin to form their first meaningful relationships and interactions with members of the opposite sex. But at this age, it can be hard to talk to someone you're interested in without sounding like a fool since the way we speak often changes as we grow older.

One of the most challenging aspects of talking with someone we're interested in is the fear of rejection. This fear can be so intense at times, oftentimes people will avoid talking to their crush entirely rather than risk saying something stupid and having them reject them or worse - laugh at them!

So it's no surprise that when we walk into a room full of strangers, our hearts start racing and we feel vulnerable and exposed without knowing what will happen next or who these people are at all. But there are ways around this fear if you want them enough! Let's get started with some strategies since the uncomfortable transition of going and approaching will eventually happen as a result of how often we do it. Let's do it with baby steps!

We begin by simply acknowledging that this fear exists. It's not something to feel guilty or ashamed about - it's natural! Whether you're introverted or extroverted, everyone feels lonely and anxious when they have to face new people. And while it can be very uncomfortable at first, eventually you'll get more comfortable around other people just like you did when you were younger.

So to get us started, let's identify the circumstances in which this fear is most prevalent. Is it only when we speak with strangers? Or maybe it happens when you speak with family members, too. All of these are possibilities that require careful examination to understand how they work and what can be done about them.

Next, how do you feel when you get this nervous? Do you get sweaty palms? A tightness in your chest? Are your feet jittery and unable to stand still? Or are you completely fine until the moment comes when someone is standing right in front of you waiting for a response or an answer? All of these sensations are important to recognize and understand.

We also need to identify what triggers this fear if it's not simply being in a new situation. For example, is it only when you're speaking with members of the opposite sex or a certain age group? Or maybe it's a particular type of person that makes you nervous such as someone who is considered attractive or in a position of authority.

When you feel this fear coming on, what do you do? Do you immediately try to get out of the situation or avoid it by saying you're sick or that something came up? Or do you jump right in and begin talking even though it's hard? Sometimes people will avoid these circumstances entirely by sitting down at the other end of the room. Or they might say something snarky to get back at their fear of feeling weak or vulnerable.

All of these are coping mechanisms that we tend to develop in childhood in response to these types of situations. But the goal is to become aware of what's happening in your mind and body when this fear arises so that you can disengage from it.

You see, the more we try to avoid it, the bigger it gets! By rewiring our minds and bodies with new habits, we're able "to modify our current response patterns and move forward in spite of fear". That is, by understanding that we're feeling this fear because we believe that we can't handle it or control the outcome.

The good news is that even if you don't want to speak with someone, all you have to do is acknowledge them and their existence. It's not easy to do but it's an option that's available. And oftentimes you can reward yourself with something sweet or interesting after you've done this.

The next level is simply making eye contact and smiling at the person who intimidates us. It helps if we can say "hello" or introduce ourselves before they come up to speak with us. As a matter of fact, to get started, challenge yourself to go out and say "Hi" or "Hey" to 5 people you walk by today with a smile. 1.) It will brighten their day and 2.) It will help you get over your fear of people. Remember, feel the fear, and take the action.

The next level is being able to carry on a conversation, even if it's just for a few minutes. If it has gone on for too long, you can say that you have more important things to do or that your friends are waiting for you somewhere else in the room. All of these are valid reasons to end a conversation.

We'll be getting more into how to have a wonderful and engaging conversation later in the book, but for now, it might be good to address some fears around conservation that have been popping up in our new digital and technological age.

Digital Communication vs. Face-to-Face Communication

The proliferation of digital devices has had a profound impact on the way we interact with each other. A recent study shows that young people are losing the ability to empathize because they rely too heavily on digital devices. The question is how much do you need to communicate with other people face to face?

Researchers observed 32 children between ages 3-6 in their homes over a period of six months. These kids were observed talking spontaneously to an adult who entered the room without any prompts or requests. The researchers also observed each child's behavior when that same adult entered the room to conduct a structured interview.

The results of this research show that children do not spontaneously interact with their parents as much as they did before digital devices became so integral in our lives. Researchers found that many of these young children have lost the ability to engage in spontaneous conversation with an adult, which is far more revealing than a structured session. For example, when given a choice between talking and playing on an iPad, the majority of kids choose the latter option over face-to-face interaction.

Researchers believe that this change is due to the fact that many children are growing up without any face-to-face interaction at all. Some of these kids seem to prefer texting over talking. These children would rather text their friends than have a live conversation, which leads to the fear of rejection or boredom with small talk so they stick with short messages instead.

Interacting with others on digital devices may also dull our ability to develop empathy skills as well, according to some studies. One study found that young people who rely on Facebook often are more narcissistic and have weaker social skills than those who do not use Facebook or other digital devices.

The main fear in face-to-face conversation, as opposed to digital communication, is that you can't edit yourself. I want to address this fear now. With digital conversation, you can edit yourself to a degree, but I have found that the more spontaneous the connection is, the easier it is to bare your soul. You might not be able to say whatever comes to mind at any given moment but you may realize a better way of phrasing something if you didn't think about it first.

Empathy and understanding are far too essential for us as human beings, therefore we must practice them in real-life interactions face-to-face, whether they're simple or challenging conversations. We must communicate with one another, therefore we should do what we can to overcome our fear of interacting with people and enjoy our time together. This is the charm of spontaneous interaction. It's made in real-time rather than at the end of a predetermined period. Because another person understands that what is said is spontaneous, they are extremely understanding.

So I'm going to give you four phrases you can use to edit yourself during a conversation that is absolutely harmless and will benefit you greatly.

1.) "Oh, sorry, that's not what I meant..."

When we're talking spontaneously, sometimes something comes out of our mouth that we didn't intend to say. We can apologize for it, and continue to carry on the conversation. Or, you can use the phrase I've given you that will not harm your conversation.

2.) "Oh, sorry, can I try that again?"

So again, it's the same concept. You're speaking off the top of your head, so anything could flow out and be delivered in an unpolished, unintentional, and even potentially disgraceful or insulting manner.

3.) "Oops, that didn't come out right. Let me rephrase..."

You go ahead and say what you actually meant to say. But this time, you make sure it's perfectly presented in a way that is accessible to whomever you're conversing with. Many writers will say that they don't know what they're thinking until they put it on paper. When you write, it's as though you are pondering on the page. And speaking in a natural face-to-face conversation is similar to real-time thinking. So the other individual, if they're a decent, average person, will understand this from their own expertise. And you simply state that you're having trouble stating what you want to say, and it may take many tries before you figure out what you mean and are successful in expressing yourself.

4.) "Oh, that sounded bad"

It happens! You say something stupid or confusing or even offensive, and now the conversation has lost its original path. Use this phrase if it happens, and you'll be able to carry on the conversation pretty well.

So next time you're really hurting for words, try using these phrases. They might not help much now, but they will later when you need them most! Then again, using the phrase itself may help enough to allow the conversation to continue without any more editing.

4

HOW TO KNOW WHAT TO SAY IN ANY SITUATION OR ENVIRONMENT

We've all been there - we're in the middle of a conversation and our mind goes blank. We can't think of what to say next and we feel embarrassed and frustrated. This can happen for a variety of reasons, such as when we're feeling stressed or when we don't know the other person very well. Maybe later in conversation, you do come up with something to say, but it's too late because the conversation is already on a different thread. And what you have to say simply isn't relevant anymore.

This can lead to you being labeled as quiet, boring, or even not interesting. It can be difficult to correct later on because you either don't know what was said in the conversation that occurred after your mind went blank or they simply no longer remember it.

So what's the solution?

First, you need to understand why your mind goes blank in conversation. That is because, when you have social anxiety, your mind frequently goes blank since you are worried about some sort of mental paralysis. Fear of public embarrassment is the most common worry. It's a fear of being recognized and ridiculed in front of others, especially people you like or don't know well, and whom you aren't too comfortable with. It's a concern about losing one's reputation. You may make yourself look foolish in a variety of ways. You can inadvertently say something ignorant or so far removed from the topic that they might perceive you as odd. You may say anything that will expose to them your lack of understanding of the subject under discussion. What you say might also suggest a lack of social interaction, which could suggest a lack of friends. For example, the group might be talking about relationships and you've never been in one. And when you make a statement that is beyond belief because of your lack of expertise, they may see right through you.

The fact is that you are scared of saying something stupid, which causes your thoughts to go blank during conversations. Realizing that we all say idiotic things and say things out of context is the key to overcoming this issue. We've all made mistakes. These blunders frequently go unnoticed. Why? Because you're not the only one who's thinking about what to say next. Other people spend a lot of time in their heads, too, considering what to say in response to what others are saying. Most of us have made a mistake at one point or another. Now, consider those who are lurking nearby and notice that you've said something out of context. The majority of them aren't concerned about whether you make a blunder.

Most of the people you encounter want you to feel at ease around them. Because if you're comfortable, so are they, and conversation will flow freely. So even if they notice that you've made a blunder, they don't make a big deal out of it. They most likely won't say anything at all. But what if they do bring it up? Simply smile and agree that it was amusing in this situation.

Demonstrate that you have a sense of humor and are comfortable with yourself by smiling at the statement. People who live their lives to the fullest make plenty of errors, even when they make a mistake. They do it all the time because they understand that this is a part of life. It's a method of learning new abilities and behaviors. It's a means to learn what doesn't work, which helps to identify what does. That's why people who make a lot of mistakes are so successful. So accept that you will make errors. Allow yourself to blurt out whatever comes to mind and say something stupid from time to time. You will see that it has little influence on your reputation. It won't reduce your standing among others in the eyes of other people.

However, it can help you develop your social abilities. Every blunder you make helps you fine-tune your social skills and makes you a better conversationalist. It will aid in your relaxation around others as long as you are willing to learn from your mistakes, accept that you will make errors, and say some things out of context. They'll notice when you don't care about making minor mistakes. You worry less, and your demeanor becomes more relaxed and collected. As a result, your conversations become more natural and your mind goes blank less frequently.

But what if this doesn't help? What if being at ease and comfortable around others doesn't help, and you still can't think of anything intelligent or unique to say?

Social anxiety, in general, keeps you from fully living your life. It prevents you from engaging in activities with other fascinating people. Hobbies that are worth discussing and might make you seem more interesting as a person. You feel like you're not an interesting individual if you don't have any interesting hobbies. As a result, you have nothing to discuss. Even when you get comfortable with someone else, you have no interesting things to say, and this can be a big problem.

The good news is that there's a very easy answer for this issue. Simply put, take an interest in others and what they have to say. Even if the person is talking about something you don't care about at the moment. Make an effort and pay attention. Become familiar with that topic so you can learn more about it. There's even a mind trick you can use that I first heard from Dr. Andrew Huberman of Huberman Lab. He said when he was in college and was in a class that bored him to death, he would repeatedly tell himself during lectures that this was the most interesting subject ever. When he sat down to do some reading for his homework or an exam, he would tell himself the same thing. As a result, he tricked his brain into paying attention and genuinely being fascinated by the subject, and a result was an A in the class.

So when it comes to having a conversation, you can convince your mind that what the other person is saying is the most interesting subject you've ever heard. Then possibly then or down the line, you actually will become genuinely interested, which opens up a whole new world in your life you would have never discovered had you not listened to that person. However, the secret is to absorb as much knowledge from other individuals as possible. By paying attention to what they have to say. Knowledge isn't just a subject like math, ethics, or anything else that can be studied in college. Everything you learn in life adds to your overall knowledge and makes you a more fascinating person. When there's something that you don't care about, but you pay attention anyhow, you gain some understanding and experience on the subject. Next time you talk about the same subject, you're not ignorant anymore. You may have a great discussion without awkward pauses just because you've been attentive in the past and genuinely interested in what others have to say.

So, ask questions and pay attention. You'll learn a lot of information over time that will make interacting with others a real joy. All you have to do now is start, and your social abilities will improve naturally.

5

HOW TO HAVE AN AMAZING CONVERSATION IN 7 STEPS

Conversations are chains. Let's picture every conversation as a tiny iron link, and as a result of each interaction with a stranger, an iron link is formed. Every discussion that follows, the link grows more solid and more robust, with each encounter we have with so many strangers, such as the barista or the Uber driver. We constantly create new links with each discussion. And in the end, we've built a vast worldwide web of conversation out of it.

When you think about it, a conversation is really an adventure. You never quite know what's going to happen. It's a chance to explore new ideas and learn about other people. It's a way to connect with the world and make new friends. It's a way to make the world a little more interesting. Conversations may be used to wage and end wars.

We all start out as strangers. We may see them on the street, or in a store, or at a party, but we don't really know them. We don't know their stories, or what they're like, or what they're thinking. We just see them as another person.

But then something happens. We decide to talk to them. And suddenly, they're not just a stranger anymore. We learn about them, and they learn about us. We share stories and experiences, and we form connections with them. We become friends, or we become enemies.

Conversations are important because they help us to connect with the world. They help us to build relationships with other people and to solve problems together. They allow us to discover new perspectives, ideas, and directions in life. They help us to build the social fabric of society.

But how do you have an amazing conversation? How can you get people to open up about themselves, and talk about their lives? How can you learn more about them while also showing that you're interesting, too? And how do you turn a chance encounter into a lifelong friendship or even something more?

Everyone and your mother told you, "Don't talk to strangers." Yes, that is certainly important advice for a child who is all alone and can be taken advantage of by a potential predator. But the advice in general, "Don't talk to strangers", is one I very much disagree with and hope to convince you to unplug from it.

Every stranger is an opportunity, a chance to learn about another person, and their own little world. They have stories to tell, perspectives worth learning from, and experiences you can gain from. And in the process of talking to them, they're also a chance for you to enhance your own life with a new friend or a great experience.

Every stranger is also an opportunity to make the world a little more interesting. Every stranger brings a new story, a novel experience, or a new way of looking at life. By talking to strangers, you can learn how to make your life better and more fulfilling.

Every stranger is also an opportunity to help someone else in their own journey through life. If you're concerned about the state of the world and other people, then conversations are a chance to help them grow, both as individuals and as part of society. By talking to strangers, you can solve complex problems that affect everyone around you, including yourself.

Now let's place ourselves in a real-world scenario that you've probably been in before.

You're at a party, and you see someone across the room that you want to talk to. But you're scared. What if they don't want to talk to you? What if they think you're weird? What if they ignore you?

These are all valid fears, but they're also fears that can be overcome. The best way to overcome them is to simply walk up to them and say hello. Maybe they don't want to talk. Oh well! They weren't talking with before, anyways. But more than likely, they will say hello back. That brings us to the first step of having an amazing conversation:

1.) Opening the Floodgates With the First Word

I truly believe that once you've said the first word, everything else will flow from there. Keep it stupid simple. Say "Hi" or "Hey" with a smile on your face. It's also important to have open and friendly body language when you do this. Here are some examples of closed or unfriendly body language:

- Crossed or folded arms
- Looking away
- Hiding the hands

Instead, use open body language such as:

- Unfolded arms
- Strong eye contact
- Visible hands
- SMILE

I know what you're thinking, what if it's just going to turn into:

'Hey, how are you?'
'Fine, you?'
'Good to hear'
'Ok, see ya'

I understand, I don't like those conversations either, and that's not what I want for you. It's a waste of your life. So here is what I'm suggesting.

2.) No small talk

Instead of making small talk, ask a very personal question. Don't be hesitant. Trust me when I say that you will be amazed at how much people are willing to tell you if you simply ask. Perhaps get any kind of personal inquiry going, such as, "Interesting name, how did your parents come up with it? What's the back story?" Or, "How long have you lived in this city?" One of my favorites is, "Where are you from?" and "Where does your family live?" This will always get the other person enthusiastic because most people are proud to talk about their origins, even if their hometown isn't all that great compared to the city they live in now. Most times, it's still the place they call home.

3.) Look for Me-Too's

Make an effort to discover anything that you and the other person have in common when you first meet someone. When you start at that point and then progress outward, the conversation will become a lot easier. The reason is you're both on the same side of something, which is a really tremendous sensation. What could you and a stranger have in common, for example? Do you both like sushi? Maybe you have similar sushi restaurant recommendations, or the other person will recommend one that you've never been to. Maybe you're both tired of the cold weather. That could lead to summer activities you both enjoy doing. The list here is truly endless. When you find a me-too, the other person is now automatically invested in the conversation.

4.) Give a One-of-a-Kind Compliment

People will forget what you do, but they will always remember how you made them feel. Be generous, and go out and give someone a wonderful compliment. Some people like to hear general compliments like, "You're beautiful" or "You're looking handsome". However, let's take the example of a supermodel who has heard "You're beautiful" a million times already this year. They've been desensitized to it. That's why it's important to give each person a unique compliment, and quite possibly one they've never heard before. Of course, don't lie! There's no need to.

5.) What's Your Opinion?

We all have opinions, and we all want them to be heard. Everyone desires affirmation, so go ahead and ask for an opinion. That's when the real conversation begins. You'll be amazed at how much you can learn about a person by asking them about something seemingly unimportant. Some people make the mistake of asking about something way too specific, like, "How do you feel about the U.S. dollar's valuation in the next 10 years?" People may get intimidated and feel like they don't know enough on the subject, and shut down. On the other hand, when you start with a simple question such as:

> "When's the last time you saw a movie? What was it?"
> "Are you reading any books right now?"
> "What's the most frustrating thing about your job?"

You're much more likely to get a response. Your conversation partner will be able to talk for 30 seconds or even 3 minutes on that topic alone! That gives you plenty of time to start up another discussion based on what they just said.

6.) Be present in the moment

Have you ever been in a conversation with someone who is constantly checking their phone, or looking around the room, as if they are waiting for something more interesting to happen? How did that make you feel? Not good, right? The best thing you can do is be present in the conversation, because this makes the other person feel special, and valued. This is important to establishing rapport with people on a deeper level. Plus, that phone can wait! Keep good eye contact with them, because it makes them feel like they're being listened to, and it keeps you from being distracted.

7.) Person, Place, and Thing

If you've ever watched the game show Wheel of Fortune, you'd know that they base their word puzzles on categories, mainly "Person, Place, and Thing." Let's start with the Person. It's so important to remember a person's name because it makes them feel special. Using someone's name in conversation is the quickest way to make friends and start meaningful relationships with people. Everyone loves to hear their own name, and when you use it they know that you really care about getting to know each other. Also, remember the places that they go or have been to. This includes places that you've both been to, and also the place that they've mentioned in the conversation. Once again, these clues help give you an idea about what makes them tick as a person. Let's not forget "Thing." This has probably already revealed itself during your first few minutes of talking to them, but keep your ears open just in case. This usually refers to a hobby or something that they're interested in, and it can turn into your next topic of conversation.

Great conversations don't just happen without any effort from both parties involved. If you consistently follow these steps while talking with another person, you will surely have a great time getting to know them!

6

TIPS FOR ASKING QUESTIONS AND LISTENING WELL

When you're interacting with someone, it's important to make them feel heard. Sometimes this means asking questions and really listening to the answers. Other times, it means paraphrasing what the other person has said to ensure you understand them correctly. By making people feel heard, you're building trust and establishing a positive relationship.

Making people feel heard is important because it makes them feel valued and appreciated. When someone takes the time to listen to us, it makes us feel like our thoughts and feelings matter. It also makes us feel like we're a part of something, that we belong. This can be important for people who may feel isolated or alone. By making people feel heard, we're giving them a valuable gift - the feeling of being understood and supported.

It can take time to get good at this. If you're not used to really listening and asking questions, it might feel awkward at first. So how can you listen well? What does it mean to ask the right questions? Here are some tips:

1. Ask open-ended questions (questions that require more than a yes/no answer)
2. Listen without judgment
3. Summarize what the other person says by repeating their main points back to them in your own words. This is called "paraphrasing." For example, if your friend tells you how much they love the new cookie shop downtown, you might say something like "Aren't those cookies the best??"
4. Respond to the emotions behind the person's words. Sometimes we communicate emotions without fully realizing it. For example, someone who says that their dog ran away may actually be saying "I feel so alone and scared," but this isn't always obvious. If you can pick up on what they're

feeling, feed those thoughts back to them in your response.

This will not only help them feel heard but also validated and understood. Here are some other examples:

> **You:** How was your weekend?
> What the other person hears: Tell me all about it! I'm really interested in you!

> **You:** How was your weekend?
> What the other person hears: I couldn't care less about you.

> **You:** How was your weekend?
> What the other person hears: Why do you insist on talking to me when all I want is for you to leave me alone? (This last one might be a bit of an exaggeration, but hopefully, it gets the point across.)

It's important to recognize that not everyone has had as much practice at active listening as others. If someone isn't good at this, they may come off as disinterested or judgmental. This can be unintentionally hurtful and make people defensive, which makes it hard for them to open up. If that's the case, you might say something like "I want to make sure I'm understanding what you're saying." It can also help if you point out specific things that they do well (e.g., "I really appreciate how much effort you put into asking me questions") so they see your perspective even though it may feel uncomfortable right now.

Interrupting Conversation

One thing that can interfere with someone feeling heard is being constantly interrupted. This can be a difficult habit to break, but it's worth it if you want to make people feel heard. Interrupting someone shows that you're not interested in what they have to say. It also makes them feel like their words are not important. As a result, the person will likely stop talking and may even start to dislike you. If you find yourself wanting to interrupt someone, try to take a step back and listen carefully to what they are saying. Maybe even repeat it back to them in your own words to make sure you understand. Only then should you offer your thoughts or ask questions.

When we express ourselves, it's important to do so in a way that feels authentic to us. This can be difficult if we're not used to it or if we're worried about how others will react. Sometimes, we might feel like we need to put on a persona or act like someone we're not in order to be taken seriously. This isn't the case. In fact, it can actually have the opposite effect. When we try too hard to be someone we're not, it's easy for people to see through it and they may even lose respect for us.

One way to express yourself confidently is to make sure that your body language is sending the right message. Are you slouching or leaning away from the person? Do you have a closed-off posture with your arms crossed? If so, it may be better to sit or stand up straighter and keep your arms at your sides. How you move can play a big role in what others think of you and how seriously they take what you say.

Talking About Yourself

When it comes to talking about ourselves, it's important to find a balance. On one hand, it's healthy to be open and share our experiences with others. On the other hand, too much self-talk can be overwhelming and off-putting.

It's not good to talk about ourselves so much because we can come across as arrogant or self-obsessed. It also makes it difficult for others to share their own stories and experiences. Plus, it can be really boring for everyone else involved! Having discussions about ourselves can make it seem like we don't care about anyone else, which is obviously not the case.

One way to strike this balance is by asking questions and listening closely. This will make others feel like they are important and that you genuinely want to hear what they have to say. In fact, when someone feels heard they tend to open up more often - so it's a win-win situation!

In summary, we all have different personalities and communication styles, but being mindful of these things can help us feel less anxious in social situations. Learning how to communicate effectively with my friends has made a big difference in my life because I've been able to create strong relationships with people who support me. By finding a balance between self-talk and listening, we can make a positive impact on the people around us.

7

DEALING WITH DIFFICULT SITUATIONS

Difficult conversations are those in which you disagree with someone or have a problem with them, but they can also be about gaining cooperation from people who don't like to work together, saying no to something that's difficult and not negotiable, and asking for help. These kinds of conversations often we go out of our way to avoid, but avoiding them usually makes things worse over time. They're particularly important because the ability to handle these conversations well is directly linked to your success at work and personal relationships. But handling them well does require careful preparation, communication skills, and the ability to de-escalate any tension that arises during the conversation. If you prepare properly, listen fully, and respond assertively you'll be able to get through difficult conversations successfully.

Most of us have some trouble with these kinds of conversations, but if you have a particularly hard time it may be because you've never thought about them in advance or had any practice with them. Take a minute and think about a recent problem you had at work. Did anything good come out of that situation? Did this person change his/her behavior as a result? If so this is proof that difficult conversations can be very effective, because they led to positive change even though they were unpleasant at first. Difficult situations are just part of life, and the skills needed to deal with them effectively are essential for your well-being and success in your work and personal relationships.

These kinds of conversations are often an opportunity. When you speak up it can lead to a better situation for you or the other person, especially if you're not trying to prove them wrong but simply share your opinion, ask for what you need, or convince someone that something is important enough to do even though it won't be convenient for them. Or perhaps they have information that will help you to understand why they're acting as they are and then things will go more smoothly between the two of you.

People who learn how to handle difficult situations well usually find that their interactions with others become easier because other people start being more cooperative and helpful. They also feel less stressed out because these kinds of conversations don't take quite as much out of them anymore. But sometimes you have to force yourself to do them even though you don't feel like it. Keep in mind, the more often you practice a new skill the easier it becomes and before long your difficult conversations will be a lot more successful and less stressful for everyone involved.

In order to handle these situations well, you need to prepare for them ahead of time so that when they come up you can speak from a place of strength instead of anxiety or frustration. The steps below are what I think are most important when preparing for a difficult conversation:

1. **Think about what's important to YOU in this situation:** The point of having difficult conversations is to get your needs met, but what you need isn't always obvious or easy

to figure out, especially when something upsetting has just happened. What matters most to you at the moment may not be what's actually most important for you in the long run, so take some time before confronting someone else involved in the situation and think through all of your options carefully so that you can speak from a place of strength instead of anger, anxiety or desperation.

2. **Decide how much is at stake:** What's at risk in this situation? Asking for what you want and presenting your point of view can feel scary when there's a lot on the line, but if you aren't willing to speak up about something that matters to you then eventually resentment will build and communication will break down completely. It's better to try and fail than not to try at all! On the other hand, some things are worth risking confrontation over, while others may be more trivial and it might be easiest just to let them go. You know what works best for you; don't let anyone else tell you otherwise.

3. **Figure out what information would help YOU move things forward:** It can be very

helpful to try and get information from other people involved in the situation to better understand where they're coming from and why they feel and act in certain ways. This allows you to see things from their perspective, which may make it easier for you to empathize with them and work together rather than against one another. However, when someone is acting controlling or manipulative it's usually not possible to have a productive conversation until they respect your right to disagree with them instead of simply trying to convince you that their way is best without any input from you at all. You might need more time alone or with close friends who will support your point of view before having this kind of conversation so that you can approach it calmly and confidently instead of feeling resentful or overwhelmed.

4. **Think about what you'll say:** Formulate your thoughts into an effective message and practice saying them out loud in front of a mirror, in a relaxed and conversational tone of voice (don't shout!) Also, think about what you'll do if things don't go your way; we

usually underestimate how willing other people are to listen when we stay calm and speak from a place of strength instead of anger or fear. There's no need to apologize for having strong feelings - expressing them is the only way that people will know how you truly feel! If someone else involved in the situation gets defensive or tries to turn it around then that tells you that they're not ready to have a respectful conversation with you yet.

5. **Plan what will happen if the discussion doesn't go YOUR way:** One of the most important things when dealing with difficult people is not to get too emotionally attached to outcomes, even when they involve your money or your career, because that means that you're bound to feel frustrated or angry whenever they don't go your way. You have no control over how someone else feels and acts, so it's up to YOU whether you allow them to take advantage of your attitude in this situation! If they're acting in a controlling or manipulative manner then it makes sense for YOU not to want anything from them until YOU are confident that

they'll respect YOU enough not to try and pressure YOU into moving things forward until YOU are ready. Remember, if you take a stand for your right to make your own decisions then other people will respect you for it and be more likely to listen when you communicate from a place of strength instead of fear or anger.

6. **Prepare for setbacks:** Sometimes standing up for yourself can backfire in unexpected ways, especially when other people involved in the situation don't see that what they're doing is hurtful or disrespectful. If this happens then try not to get angry or resentful, but use it as an opportunity to be clear about how their behavior makes you feel and also tell them why it's important to respect YOUR boundaries. People who love, like, and respect you want to know how to take care of you and will be more likely to listen when you explain it to them calmly and firmly instead of getting upset or angry.

7. **Pick the best time and place:** Once things have settled down a bit, such as after work or on another evening, choose a time and place for the conversation where both of you

can speak openly without distractions. If possible, talk in person rather than over text messages or social media because that way there's less room for misunderstandings about the tone of voice! It usually works best if someone who isn't involved in the situation acts as a mediator between both parties so that they can keep everything fair and equal by asking each person what THEIR point of view is before allowing either party to respond.

8. **Stick to facts, not feelings:** If you keep emotions out of it then it makes it easier for the other person to stay calm and open-minded because they're focusing on information rather than reacting to how they feel about what you have to say. Remember that people who care about you will want to know how their actions affect YOU so that they can change or stop doing them if necessary! For example, instead of saying something vague like "I feel disrespected" try being clear by describing exactly WHY you felt uncomfortable with something they said or did.

9. **Put yourself in their shoes:** Before having

the conversation with someone else, spend a little time thinking about why THEY might be acting or feeling way. This isn't an excuse to treat them unfairly, but it does mean that you should at least try and see things from their perspective. This might help you think of less hurtful ways to bring up difficult topics, while also making you feel more compassionate and understanding about what they're going through!

10. **Be willing to compromise:** Even though this isn't your fault, if someone else involved in the situation is taking advantage of YOUR willingness to listen then it's your responsibility to make sure that YOU feel respected too! If the other person is on board - great; if not - then set a limit on how much time or energy YOU are willing to spend dealing with THEIR issues (ie. "I care about our friendship so I'll give you two chances to talk about this, but after that I'm going to go do something else until you're feeling better.")

11. **Follow-up:** This is a good way of letting the other person know that you still care even if they don't want to talk about your difficult

situation right now. They might be thinking things through while they aren't around, or maybe they just need some time to process it on their own before discussing further! In any case, following up lets them know that YOU are willing to make an effort for THEIR sake, too.

CONCLUSION

The problem of being shy is that shy people often find it difficult to initiate and carry out conversations with others. This can lead to feelings of loneliness and isolation, as well as a lack of social support. Fortunately, the problem is easily rectifiable. The solution to this problem can be found in a simple conversation guide that anyone can memorize and apply when necessary. Using The Art of Conversation and its many suggestions and strategies, it's possible to overcome shyness and become more confident at talking with others.

Many strategies can be used to overcome shyness. One such strategy is to make a conscious effort to be more social. This can be done by seeking out social activities, or by making an effort to talk to others even when you don't feel like it. Another strategy is to focus on your strengths. When you feel shy, try to think about the things that you're good at, and focus on those things when speaking with others. Additionally, it's important to be yourself. Trying to be someone that you're not will only make you feel more shy and uncomfortable. Finally, practice makes perfect. The more you engage in conversations, the more comfortable you'll become.

I hope that this book has helped you to see that social anxiety and shyness do not have to define who you are. You can take the steps necessary to overcome your fear of talking to other people, and in doing so, you will find that your life opens up in ways you never thought possible. The world is full of interesting, wonderful people just waiting to meet you; don't let shyness keep you from experiencing all that life has to offer. I want nothing more than for every reader of this book to be able to confidently walk into any social situation and connect with others on a deeper level.

Made in the USA
Monee, IL
15 August 2022